Shri Krishna Janmabhoomi "Dispute for land"

Swatantra Bahadur

Published by Swatantra Bahadur, 2024.

Disclaimer

Shri Krishna Janmabhoomi "Dispute for land"

First edition. **March 15, 2024.**

Copyright © **2024** Swatantra Bahadur.

Written by **Swatantra Bahadur**

Editor - **Mahima Tripathi**

Website - Bookwisehub.com

Contents

D. International reactions or involvement

VIII. Conclusion

A. Summarize key points

B. Highlight the ongoing significance of Krishna Janmabhumi in contemporary times.

Introduction

In the sacred tapestry of Hindu mythology and religious lore, few narratives resonate as profoundly as the story of Krishna Janmabhoomi. This hallowed land, nestled in the heart of Mathura, carries the echoes of divine footsteps, marking the birthplace of Lord Krishna, a revered deity whose life and teachings have transcended millennia. As we embark on a journey through the pages of this book, we delve into the rich tapestry of Krishna Janmabhoomi, exploring its mythical origins, historical significance, and the complex interplay of faith and contested heritage.

This book seeks to unravel the layers of devotion and discord that enshroud Krishna Janmabhoomi, tracing the footsteps of the divine child born amidst the serenity of Mathura's landscape. As we navigate the contours of this sacred terrain, we encounter the ruins of a once-standing temple, witness the construction of the Shahi Idgah Mosque, and grapple with the longstanding dispute that has woven itself into the fabric of Hindu-Muslim relations.

The narrative unfolds not merely as a historical chronicle but as a testament to the enduring human quest for the divine and the perpetual struggles for coexistence in a diverse and pluralistic society. Through meticulous examination, we aim to present a comprehensive case study that delves into the legal battles, archaeological explorations, and the socio-political dynamics that have defined the journey of Krishna Janmabhoomi from antiquity to the present day.

As the tendrils of time connect the ancient to the contemporary, this book endeavors to provide readers with a nuanced understanding of the complexities surrounding Krishna Janmabhoomi. It invites contemplation on the intersections of faith, heritage, and identity while encouraging a dialogue that transcends the confines of historical disputes. In navigating the intricate web of beliefs and controversies, we embark on a quest to decipher the cultural and spiritual tapestry that continues to shape the contours of Krishna Janmabhoomi.

A. Brief overview of Krishna Janmabhumi

Krishna Janmabhumi, translated as the "Birthplace of Lord Krishna," stands as a revered pilgrimage site in the ancient city of Mathura, Uttar Pradesh, India. Enshrined in Hindu mythology and tradition, this sacred land holds profound significance as the birthplace of Lord Krishna, a deity whose life and teachings are chronicled in the epic Mahabharata and the Bhagavad Gita.

Mathura, nestled on the banks of the Yamuna River, is believed to be the sacred ground where Lord Krishna made his divine appearance thousands of years ago. The spiritual aura of Krishna Janmabhumi resonates with devotees and pilgrims who flock to this hallowed ground seeking blessings and a connection with the revered deity.

The sanctity of Krishna Janmabhumi is heightened by the existence of ancient temples and sacred structures that pay homage to Lord Krishna. However, the site is not only a repository of religious fervor but has also become entangled in historical and legal disputes, adding layers of complexity to its narrative.

As we embark on a journey to explore Krishna Janmabhumi, we encounter not just the celestial tales of Lord Krishna's birth but also the intricate interplay of faith, history, and controversies that have shaped its identity over the centuries. This brief overview serves as a portal into the captivating realm of Krishna Janmabhumi, inviting readers to delve deeper into the multifaceted tapestry of its existence.

B. Significance in Hindu mythology and religious beliefs

The significance of Krishna Janmabhumi in Hindu mythology and religious beliefs is deeply ingrained in the cultural and spiritual fabric of India. It serves as a focal point for devotees and pilgrims, symbolizing the divine birth of Lord Krishna, one of the most revered and beloved deities in Hinduism. The following points highlight the profound importance of Krishna Janmabhoomi.

Divine Birth of Lord Krishna: According to Hindu scriptures, especially the Bhagavad Gita and the Mahabharata, Lord Krishna is considered the eighth incarnation (avatar) of Lord Vishnu. His birth at Mathura's Krishna Janmabhoomi is celebrated as a divine event, marking the intervention of the divine in human form to restore righteousness (dharma) and guide humanity.

Cultural Heritage: Krishna Janmabhumi is not only a religious site but also a cultural treasure trove. It preserves and showcases the rich cultural heritage associated with Lord Krishna's life, providing a platform for artistic expressions, music, dance, and rituals that celebrate the deity's divine exploits.

Pilgrimage Destination: Millions of pilgrims undertake journeys to Krishna Janmabhumi to seek spiritual solace and divine blessings. The pilgrimage is not just a physical journey but also a metaphorical one, reflecting the devotees' quest for a deeper connection with the divine and a pursuit of spiritual enlightenment.

Devotional Practices: Temples and shrines at Krishna Janmabhoomi are centers of devotional practices, including singing bhajans (devotional songs), reciting scriptures, and participating in religious ceremonies. These practices foster a sense of unity among devotees and strengthen their bond with Lord Krishna.

Festivals and Celebrations: The annual celebration of Janmashtami, Lord Krishna's birthday, transforms Krishna Janmabhumi into a vibrant center of festivities. Devotees engage in elaborate rituals, processions, and cultural events, enhancing the site's significance during this auspicious occasion.

Symbol of Love and Compassion: Lord Krishna's teachings, especially those found in the Bhagavad Gita, emphasize love, righteousness, and compassion. Krishna Janmabhumi, as the birthplace of this divine teacher, symbolizes these values and serves as an inspiration for devotees to incorporate them into their lives.

Krishna Janmabhoomi holds immense significance in Hindu mythology and religious beliefs, serving as a sacred nexus between the celestial and the earthly realms. It stands as a testament to the enduring cultural and spiritual heritage that continues to captivate the hearts and minds of millions of devotees across the world.

II. Story of Krishna Janmabhoomi

The story of Krishna Janmabhoomi is deeply ingrained in Hindu mythology, tracing its roots to the revered texts of ancient India, particularly the Bhagavad Gita and the Mahabharata. At the heart of this narrative is the divine figure of Lord Krishna, one of the most worshiped deities in Hinduism, and the events surrounding his birth in the sacred city of Mathura.

According to Hindu scriptures, Lord Krishna was born in the Dwapara Yuga, an epoch characterized by grandeur and cosmic significance. His parents, Vasudeva and Devaki, were imprisoned by Devaki's brother, the tyrant King Kansa, due to a prophetic prediction that Kansa would be killed by Devaki's eighth son.

In captivity, as the oppression of the tyrant continued, Lord Krishna manifested a divine plan. On the stormy night of his birth, the prison doors miraculously opened, and Vasudeva, guided by divine intervention, carried the infant Krishna across the raging Yamuna River to Gokul, where he was placed in the care of Nanda and Yashoda, a cowherd couple.

The city of Mathura, where Krishna was born, is considered a sacred pilgrimage site and is revered as Krishna Janmabhoomi. The prison cell, known as the "Krishna Janmasthan," is believed to be the exact spot where Lord Krishna made his divine appearance.

The childhood exploits of Krishna, including his playful pranks (known as "leelas") and profound teachings in the Bhagavad Gita, have further elevated the significance of Krishna Janmabhoomi in Hindu religious beliefs. The stories of Krishna's divine interventions, his love for the gopis (milkmaids), and his role as a charismatic leader during the Mahabharata war contribute to the multifaceted tapestry of Krishna's mythology.

Devotees from across the world visit Krishna Janmabhoomi to immerse themselves in the divine energy of Lord Krishna's birthplace, seeking blessings, spiritual solace, and a profound connection with the timeless tales that continue to resonate through the ages.

A. Mythological narratives surrounding Lord Krishna's birth

The mythological narratives surrounding Lord Krishna's birth are richly woven into the fabric of Hindu scriptures, captivating the hearts and minds of millions of devotees. According to the Bhagavad Gita, the Mahabharata, and the Puranas, the story of Lord Krishna's birth unfolds with cosmic significance and divine interventions.

Prophecy and Imprisonment:

The saga begins with a divine prophecy foretelling the downfall of the tyrant King Kansa, Devaki's brother. It was predicted that Kansa would meet his end at the hands of Devaki's eighth son. Disturbed by this prophecy, Kansa imprisons Devaki and her husband Vasudeva to thwart any potential threat.

The Divine Birth:

As Kansa mercilessly imprisons his sister, a series of miraculous events unfold during the birth of Lord Krishna. Devaki and Vasudeva, despite their captivity, find solace in the divine presence of Lord Vishnu, who assures them of their child's protection. When Krishna is born, the prison doors miraculously open, and Vasudeva is guided to carry the infant across the stormy Yamuna River to the safety of Gokul.

Exchange with Yashoda:

In Gokul, Vasudeva places baby Krishna beside Yashoda's newborn daughter. When Kansa attempts to slay the child, a celestial voice warns him that his nemesis is still alive. Realizing the divine exchange, Kansa intensifies his pursuit of Krishna.

Childhood Exploits (Leelas):

The tales of Krishna's childhood, filled with enchanting leelas or divine pastimes, depict him as a mischievous yet divine child. These stories include Krishna's playful interactions with the gopis, his encounters with demons sent by Kansa, and his endearing bond with the residents of Gokul.

Mahabharata and the Bhagavad Gita:

The narrative extends to Krishna's role as a pivotal figure in the Mahabharata. He serves as the charioteer and advisor to Prince Arjuna during the great war of Kurukshetra. It is on the battlefield that Krishna imparts the profound teachings of the Bhagavad Gita, addressing fundamental questions of duty, righteousness, and the path to spiritual realization.

The mythological narratives surrounding Lord Krishna's birth, characterized by divine interventions, celestial prophecies, and the embodiment of compassion, continue to resonate in the hearts of devotees, making Krishna Janmabhoomi a sacred pilgrimage site and Lord Krishna a cherished deity in Hinduism.

B. Historical significance of Mathura as Krishna's birthplace

Mathura, one of the oldest cities in India, holds immense historical significance as the birthplace of Lord Krishna. Situated on the banks of the Yamuna River in the northern state of Uttar Pradesh, Mathura has been a cradle of ancient Indian civilization, art, and spirituality.

Historically, Mathura was a thriving center of trade and culture, dating back to the Vedic period. Its association with Lord Krishna further elevated its importance as a sacred city. The tangible link to Lord Krishna's birth is evident in the presence of the Krishna Janmabhoomi, the prison cell where he is believed to have been born.

Over the centuries, Mathura has witnessed the rise and fall of various empires, including the Mauryas, Kushans, and Guptas, each leaving its imprint on the city's cultural landscape. The city's temples and sacred sites dedicated to Lord Krishna attract pilgrims and devotees from around the world, contributing to Mathura's enduring status as a revered pilgrimage destination.

The historical significance of Mathura extends beyond the celestial tales, encompassing its role as a cradle of ancient Indian civilization and spirituality. Today, the city stands as a testament to the confluence of myth and history, where the divine and earthly realms converge in the sacred land of Lord Krishna's birth.

III. Demolished Temple for Shahi Idgah Mosque

The story of the demolished temple for the Shahi Idgah Mosque traces back to a historical period marked by religious and political turbulence. It revolves around the construction of the Shahi Idgah Mosque in the city of Mathura, Uttar Pradesh, India, and the preceding demolition of a Hindu temple that once stood on the same site.

Background:

In 1669, during the reign of the Mughal Emperor Aurangzeb, a grand mosque named Shahi Idgah was built in Mathura. However, the construction of this mosque involved the demolition of a pre-existing Hindu temple that is believed to have been dedicated to Lord Krishna. This act of demolition reflects a complex interplay of religious and political dynamics prevalent during the Mughal era.

Controversies Surrounding the Demolition:

The demolition of the temple for the Shahi Idgah Mosque has been a source of historical controversy and contention. The act symbolizes a chapter in India's history marked by religious iconoclasm, where structures of worship from diverse faiths were often targeted for political reasons. The destruction of the temple in Mathura is viewed by some as a representation of the religious intolerance that prevailed during certain periods of Mughal rule.

Impact on Communal Relations:

The historical demolition and subsequent construction have had a lasting impact on Hindu-Muslim relations in the region. The contentious history of the site has fueled communal tensions and contributed to a broader discourse on religious coexistence. The dispute over the temple's demolition and the construction of the mosque has become a symbol of the historical complexities that continue to influence interfaith relationships in contemporary times.

Ongoing Controversy:

The controversy surrounding the demolished temple for the Shahi Idgah Mosque persists to this day. Legal battles and disputes over the ownership and status of the site have been ongoing, with various stakeholders representing both the Hindu and Muslim communities. The complex nature of the case reflects the challenges in reconciling historical grievances with the principles of religious harmony and coexistence.

The story of the demolished temple for the Shahi Idgah Mosque serves as a poignant reminder of the historical intricacies that shape the cultural and religious landscape of the region, while also highlighting the need for respectful dialogue and understanding among different communities.

A. Historical background of the temple

The historical background of the temple that stood at the site later occupied by the Shahi Idgah Mosque in Mathura is rooted in the rich tapestry of India's ancient history and religious heritage.

Ancient Roots:

Mathura has been a sacred city for Hindus since ancient times, and historical records indicate that it was a thriving cultural and religious center. The city is associated with the life and teachings of Lord Krishna, who is revered as one of the principal deities in Hinduism. Temples dedicated to Lord Krishna were constructed in Mathura to commemorate his divine presence and significant life events, including his birth.

Krishna Janmabhumi:

The specific historical background of the temple in question is often tied to the broader narrative of Krishna Janmabhumi, the purported birthplace of Lord Krishna. The area around the Krishna Janmabhumi is believed to have hosted temples dedicated to the worship of Lord Krishna for centuries. Devotees regarded this site with deep reverence, and the temples were essential pilgrimage destinations.

Mughal Era and Aurangzeb's Reign:

The Mughal Emperor Aurangzeb, who ruled from 1658 to 1707, was known for his strict interpretation of Islamic law and his policies against non-Muslim religious structures. During his reign, several Hindu temples were targeted for demolition, and mosques were constructed in their stead. The temple that once stood at the site of the Shahi Idgah Mosque in Mathura was one such casualty of this policy.

DESTRUCTION AND CONSTRUCTION:

In 1669, the construction of the Shahi Idgah Mosque led to the demolition of the Hindu temple that occupied the same space. The historical background of the temple becomes a significant chapter in the broader context of religious iconoclasm during the Mughal era. The act of demolishing religious structures from one faith to make way for another was reflective of the political and religious dynamics of the time.

Understanding the historical background of the temple provides crucial context to the complexities and controversies surrounding the site in contemporary times. It sheds light on the layers of religious, cultural, and political history that have shaped the region and contributed to ongoing debates and legal disputes regarding the Shahi Idgah Mosque and the historical temple that once stood in its place.

<u>B. Construction of the Shahi Idgah Mosque and demolition of the temple</u>

The construction of the Shahi Idgah Mosque in Mathura and the simultaneous demolition of the Hindu temple on the same site is a historical episode that unfolded during the reign of the Mughal Emperor Aurangzeb in the 17th century.

1. Reign of Aurangzeb:

During Aurangzeb's rule (1658–1707), the Mughal Empire experienced a shift towards a more orthodox interpretation of Islam. Aurangzeb, known for his austere lifestyle and strict adherence to Islamic principles, initiated policies that targeted non-Muslim religious structures, including Hindu temples.

2. Temple Destruction Policy:

As part of Aurangzeb's policy against non-Muslim places of worship, a significant number of Hindu temples were demolished, and mosques were erected in their place. The policy aimed to enforce a more puritanical form of Islam and asserted the dominance of the ruling power.

3. Construction of Shahi Idgah Mosque:

In 1669, the Shahi Idgah Mosque was constructed in Mathura on a site that was believed to have been the location of a prominent Hindu temple. The mosque was built on the orders of Aurangzeb and served as a place for Muslims to gather and offer prayers during the Eid al-Adha festival.

4. Demolition of the Hindu Temple:

The construction of the Shahi Idgah Mosque involved the demolition of the pre-existing Hindu temple that once stood on the site. The temple, likely dedicated to Lord Krishna, was razed to the ground, symbolizing the policy of religious iconoclasm that characterized Aurangzeb's rule.

5. Impact on the Local Community:

The demolition of the temple had a profound impact on the local Hindu community. It led to a rupture in the sacred landscape of Mathura, a city deeply rooted in Hindu mythology and religious traditions. The act of replacing a Hindu temple with a mosque became emblematic of the religious tensions and cultural clashes of the time.

The construction of the Shahi Idgah Mosque and the demolition of the temple represent a historical chapter marked by religious intolerance and iconoclastic policies. The echoes of this event continue to reverberate in contemporary debates and legal disputes surrounding the Shahi Idgah Mosque and the historical temple in Mathura.

C. CONTROVERSIES SURROUNDING the mosque's construction

The construction of the Shahi Idgah Mosque in Mathura, coupled with the demolition of the pre-existing Hindu temple, has been shrouded in controversies that persist through the annals of history. The events surrounding the mosque's construction have sparked debates, legal disputes, and communal tensions, adding layers of complexity to the already sensitive issue.

1. Religious Iconoclasm:

The construction of the Shahi Idgah Mosque is emblematic of a broader policy of religious iconoclasm pursued by Emperor Aurangzeb during the Mughal era. This policy, aimed at promoting a more orthodox form of Islam, led to the demolition of several Hindu temples, with the Shahi Idgah Mosque in Mathura being a prominent example.

2. Cultural and Historical Heritage:

The controversy extends to the impact on the cultural and historical heritage of Mathura. The city is revered as the birthplace of Lord Krishna, and the presence of ancient temples attested to its rich cultural and religious legacy. The construction of the mosque, resulting in the destruction of a temple, stirred sentiments related to the preservation of cultural heritage.

3. Communal Tensions:

The controversies surrounding the mosque's construction have had enduring implications on Hindu-Muslim relations in the region. The act of demolishing a Hindu temple and replacing it with a mosque became a focal point for communal tensions, leaving a lasting impact on the social fabric of Mathura.

4. Legal Disputes:

Over the years, the construction of the Shahi Idgah Mosque has become entangled in legal disputes. Ownership and the status of the site have been subjects of legal battles, with various parties representing both Hindu and Muslim communities presenting their claims and counterclaims.

5. Contemporary Debates:

The controversies surrounding the mosque's construction continue to resonate in contemporary times. The debates often transcend legal dimensions and delve into broader discussions about religious harmony, cultural preservation, and the need for respectful dialogue between different religious communities.

6. Impact on Interfaith Relations:

The construction of the Shahi Idgah Mosque has left an enduring impact on interfaith relations. The contested history of the site has posed challenges in fostering mutual understanding and cooperation between Hindus and Muslims in the region.

In summary, the controversies surrounding the construction of the Shahi Idgah Mosque in Mathura are multi-faceted, touching upon religious, cultural, legal, and social dimensions. The events of the past continue to shape the narratives and perspectives that influence discussions around the site in the present day.

IV. Dispute Between Hindu-Muslim

The dispute between Hindus and Muslims, particularly concerning religious sites, has been a persistent and complex issue in the Indian subcontinent. One of the prominent instances that encapsulates the intricacies of this dispute is the longstanding conflict over the Krishna Janmabhoomi in Mathura, Uttar Pradesh. This dispute reflects historical grievances, religious sentiments, legal complexities, and the broader challenge of navigating communal relations in a diverse society.

The roots of the Hindu-Muslim dispute in Mathura trace back to the Mughal era when Emperor Aurangzeb, known for his strict Islamic policies, ordered the construction of the Shahi Idgah Mosque in 1669. This mosque was built on the site believed to be the birthplace of Lord Krishna, a revered deity in Hinduism. The construction involved the demolition of an existing Hindu temple, sparking tensions that would echo through the centuries.

The dispute revolves around the assertion by Hindu groups that the mosque was built on the ruins of a Hindu temple dedicated to Lord Krishna. The significance of Mathura as the birthplace of Lord Krishna adds a profound religious and cultural dimension to the conflict. Hindu devotees hold a deep emotional connection to the Krishna Janmabhoomi, considering it a sacred pilgrimage site.

Legal battles have been a defining feature of this dispute, with multiple cases filed over the years to establish the rightful ownership and status of the site. The legal complexities are compounded by the lack of definitive historical evidence and the challenge of reconciling faith with legal principles. The Ayodhya verdict in 2019, which favored the construction of a Ram temple on the disputed site in Ayodhya, further fueled discussions and expectations surrounding other contested religious sites, including Mathura.

The dispute has not only played out in courts but has also manifested in public sentiments and political discourse. The Krishna Janmabhoomi issue, much like the Ayodhya dispute, has become a rallying point for various political and religious groups. The intensity of emotions surrounding these disputes reflects the deep-seated connections between religious identity and political mobilization in India.

Despite the complexities and controversies, there have been attempts at resolution and dialogue. Interfaith initiatives, involving leaders from both Hindu and Muslim communities, have sought to promote understanding and peaceful coexistence. However, progress has been slow, with the historical grievances and the weight of the past hindering swift resolution.

The Krishna Janmabhoomi dispute underscores the broader challenge of fostering communal harmony in a nation known for its religious and cultural diversity. It prompts reflections on the delicate balance between preserving cultural heritage and accommodating the rights and sentiments of various religious communities. The resolution of such disputes requires a nuanced approach, one that acknowledges historical realities, respects religious sentiments, and promotes an inclusive vision for the future.

In conclusion, the dispute between Hindus and Muslims over the Krishna Janmabhoomi in Mathura encapsulates the multifaceted nature of religious conflicts in India. It reflects the intricate interplay of history, faith, legal intricacies, and political dynamics. As the nation grapples with these challenges, the journey towards a harmonious coexistence remains a work in progress, shaped by the collective efforts of individuals, communities, and the institutions that seek to bridge divides and build a shared understanding.

A. Overview of the longstanding dispute

The Krishna Janmabhoomi dispute stands as a poignant reflection of the complex and longstanding tensions between Hindus and Muslims in India. This protracted and emotionally charged dispute centers around the revered city of Mathura in Uttar Pradesh, where the birthplace of Lord Krishna, a highly venerated deity in Hinduism, is believed to be located. The roots of this dispute delve into historical, religious, and legal realms, making it a microcosm of the broader challenges faced by a diverse and pluralistic society.

The historical backdrop of the dispute dates back to the Mughal era during the reign of Emperor Aurangzeb in the 17th century. Aurangzeb, known for his austere interpretation of Islam, ordered the construction of the Shahi Idgah Mosque in Mathura in 1669. This mosque was built on the site where a Hindu temple, supposedly dedicated to Lord Krishna, had previously stood. The act of demolishing the temple to make way for the mosque marked the beginning of the tensions that would echo through centuries.

The core contention lies in the assertion by Hindu groups that the Shahi Idgah Mosque was constructed on the ruins of the ancient Hindu temple, the Krishna Janmabhoomi. The religious significance of Mathura as the birthplace of Lord Krishna makes the dispute emotionally charged for millions of Hindus who consider the site sacred. The clash between historical narratives and religious beliefs forms the foundation of the ongoing dispute.

Legal battles have played a pivotal role in shaping the trajectory of the Krishna Janmabhoomi conflict. Multiple court cases have been filed over the years, each seeking to establish the rightful ownership and status of the disputed site. However, the lack of definitive historical evidence and the challenge of reconciling faith with legal principles have added layers of complexity to the legal proceedings. The legal terrain became even more intricate after the landmark Ayodhya verdict in 2019, which granted permission for the construction of a Ram temple at the disputed site in Ayodhya. The Ayodhya verdict has spurred discussions and expectations regarding other contested religious sites, including Mathura.

The dispute has not only unfolded within the courtroom but has permeated public sentiments and political discourse. The Krishna Janmabhoomi issue, similar to the Ayodhya dispute, has become a rallying point for various political and religious groups. The intensity of emotions surrounding these disputes reflects the deep-seated connections between religious identity and political mobilization in India.

Attempts at resolution and dialogue have been made over the years, involving leaders from both Hindu and Muslim communities. Interfaith initiatives seek to promote understanding and peaceful coexistence, recognizing the need for a harmonious solution to this deeply rooted conflict. However, progress has been slow, as historical grievances and the weight of the past continue to hinder a swift and amicable resolution.

The Krishna Janmabhoomi dispute underscores the broader challenge of fostering communal harmony in a nation celebrated for its religious and cultural diversity. It prompts reflections on the delicate balance between preserving cultural heritage and accommodating the rights and sentiments of various religious communities. As the nation grapples with these challenges, the Krishna Janmabhoomi dispute remains an emblematic testament to the ongoing journey towards building understanding and forging a shared vision for a diverse and harmonious society.

C. Legal battles and court cases related to Krishna Janmabhoomi

The legal battles and court cases related to the Krishna Janmabhoomi dispute have been pivotal in shaping the narrative surrounding the contested site in Mathura. This complex and longstanding legal journey involves efforts from both Hindu and Muslim communities to establish their claims, presenting a multifaceted examination of historical, religious, and legal dimensions.

The legal saga commenced with a series of cases seeking to determine the rightful ownership and status of the disputed site. The first significant legal battle took place in 1968 when a civil suit was filed by the Shri Krishna Janmasthan Seva Sansthan, a Hindu trust, in the Mathura District Court. The suit sought the removal of the Idgah Mosque and the restoration of the site to Hindu ownership, contending that the mosque had been built on the ruins of a Hindu temple.

The legal proceedings gained momentum over the years, with subsequent cases filed in various courts. The complexities of the Krishna Janmabhoomi dispute were exacerbated by the absence of concrete historical evidence, adding layers of intricacy to the legal arguments presented by both parties.

The contentious nature of the dispute led to the filing of a suit in the Mathura District Court in 1970 on behalf of the Shahi Idgah Management Committee, representing the Muslim community. This suit aimed to establish the legal rights of Muslims over the disputed site and contested the claims made by the Hindu trust.

The legal landscape underwent a significant shift in 1989 when a local judge ruled in favor of the Hindus, ordering the removal of a mosque that stood adjacent to the Krishna Janmabhoomi. However, this decision was later overturned by the Allahabad High Court in 1992, citing procedural irregularities.

The dispute took a new turn in 1993 when the Indian government, led by then-Prime Minister P.V. Narasimha Rao, enacted the Acquisition of Certain Area at Ayodhya Act. This legislation sought to acquire the disputed land in Ayodhya and Mathura and maintain the status quo, freezing the legal status of both sites.

In the following years, legal battles continued as various parties filed appeals and counter-appeals in higher courts. The legal proceedings in the Krishna Janmabhoomi dispute remained entangled with the broader legal landscape surrounding religious sites in India.

The Ayodhya verdict in 2019, which granted permission for the construction of a Ram temple at the disputed site in Ayodhya, reignited discussions and expectations surrounding other contested religious sites, including Mathura. This landmark judgment has implications for the legal trajectory of the Krishna Janmabhoomi dispute, as it sets a precedent for the resolution of such complex and emotionally charged cases.

As of the latest available information, the legal battles over the Krishna Janmabhoomi dispute continue, with parties from both communities presenting their arguments and evidence. The delicate task of balancing historical claims with legal principles remains at the forefront, emphasizing the need for a nuanced and equitable resolution to this longstanding dispute. The legal journey of the Krishna Janmabhoomi dispute serves as a testament to the intricate intersections of law, history, and faith in the Indian context.

D. Impact on communal harmony and societal relations

The Krishna Janmabhoomi dispute has had a profound impact on communal harmony and societal relations in the region, reflecting the broader challenges of navigating religious diversity in India. The emotive and historically charged nature of the dispute has contributed to communal tensions, fostering a climate where delicate interfaith relationships are tested.

1. COMMUNAL TENSIONS:

The Krishna Janmabhoomi dispute has been a source of heightened communal tensions between Hindus and Muslims. The contestation over the sacred site, coupled with historical grievances and religious sentiments, has at times led to outbreaks of violence and strained relations between the two communities. Incidents of communal strife often escalate during significant legal developments or heightened public discourse surrounding the dispute.

2. Polarization:

The dispute has, over time, contributed to societal polarization along religious lines. It has become a symbolic issue that political and religious leaders sometimes exploit to further their agendas, deepening the divisions between communities. This polarization undermines the fabric of social cohesion, making it challenging for communities to engage in constructive dialogue and mutual understanding.

3. Trust Deficit:

The protracted legal battles and contested history surrounding the Krishna Janmabhoomi dispute have led to a significant trust deficit between Hindus and Muslims in the region. The lack of resolution and the uncertainty surrounding the site contribute to suspicions and apprehensions on both sides, hindering the development of trust and collaboration between communities.

4. Social Cohesion Challenges:

The persistent nature of the dispute has posed challenges to social cohesion in Mathura and its surrounding areas. It has created an atmosphere where communities may be hesitant to engage with each other openly, fearing potential repercussions or misunderstandings. This erosion of social cohesion undermines the principles of a harmonious and inclusive society.

5. Impact on Local Economy:

The prolonged dispute also has economic ramifications for the local community. The uncertainty surrounding the Krishna Janmabhoomi site can deter potential investors, tourists, and businesses, affecting the overall economic development of the region. This economic impact further compounds the challenges faced by the local population.

6. POLITICAL EXPLOITATION:

The Krishna Janmabhoomi dispute has often been exploited for political gains, with various political entities seeking to leverage the emotive issue to mobilize support from their respective constituencies. This political exploitation further exacerbates tensions and hampers genuine efforts to foster communal harmony.

7. Need for Dialogue and Understanding:

The impact of the Krishna Janmabhoomi dispute underscores the urgent need for sustained efforts toward interfaith dialogue, understanding, and reconciliation. Initiatives that encourage communities to engage in open and respectful conversations can play a crucial role in mitigating tensions and fostering a sense of shared citizenship.

8. Potential for Coexistence:

Despite the challenges, there is also potential for communities to coexist harmoniously. Grassroots initiatives that promote cultural exchange, shared traditions, and mutual respect can contribute to bridging the divide. Local leaders, community organizations, and religious figures can play pivotal roles in fostering an environment of unity and understanding.

In conclusion, the Krishna Janmabhoomi dispute has left a lasting imprint on communal harmony and societal relations in the region. While it has tested the fabric of coexistence, there remains an opportunity for communities to work collaboratively toward a shared future. Efforts toward dialogue, understanding, and economic development can help pave the way for a more harmonious and inclusive society in Mathura and beyond.

V. Case Study of Janmabhoomi

The Krishna Janmabhoomi case is a poignant and complex legal dispute centered around the birthplace of Lord Krishna in the city of Mathura, Uttar Pradesh, India. This case study delves into the historical, religious, and legal dimensions of the dispute, examining its evolution, key events, and the broader implications on communal relations and societal harmony.

Background:

The roots of the Krishna Janmabhoomi dispute trace back to the Mughal era, specifically during the reign of Emperor Aurangzeb in the 17th century. In 1669, the Shahi Idgah Mosque was constructed in Mathura, and historical records suggest that it involved the demolition of a pre-existing Hindu temple, believed to be the birthplace of Lord Krishna.

Legal Battles and Key Cases:

1968 Civil Suit: The legal battles began in 1968 when the Shri Krishna Janmasthan Seva Sansthan, a Hindu trust, filed a civil suit in the Mathura District Court. The suit sought the removal of the Shahi Idgah Mosque and the restoration of the site to Hindu ownership. The claim was based on the assertion that the mosque had been built on the ruins of a Hindu temple.

1970 Counter Suit: In response, a counter-suit was filed in 1970 on behalf of the Shahi Idgah Management Committee, representing the Muslim community. This suit sought to establish the legal rights of

Muslims over the disputed site and contested the claims made by the Hindu trust.

1989 Mathura District Court Ruling: In 1989, a local judge ruled in favor of the Hindus, ordering the removal of a mosque adjacent to the Krishna Janmabhoomi. However, this decision was subsequently overturned by the Allahabad High Court in 1992, citing procedural irregularities.

1993 Acquisition of Certain Area at Ayodhya Act: The Indian government, led by Prime Minister P.V. Narasimha Rao, enacted the Acquisition of Certain Area at Ayodhya Act in 1993. This legislation aimed to acquire the disputed land in Ayodhya and Mathura, freezing the legal status of both sites and maintaining the status quo.

Post-Ayodhya Verdict Developments: The Ayodhya verdict in 2019, which favored the construction of a Ram temple at the disputed site in Ayodhya, reignited discussions and expectations surrounding other contested religious sites, including Mathura. The Krishna Janmabhoomi dispute gained renewed attention in the context of the Ayodhya judgment.

Impact on Communal Harmony and Societal Relations:

The Krishna Janmabhoomi dispute has had far-reaching implications on communal relations and societal harmony. The emotive and contested nature of the case has been a source of heightened communal tensions, contributing to societal polarization along religious lines. The lack of resolution and the uncertainty surrounding the site have led to a significant trust deficit between Hindus and Muslims in the region. The dispute has also been exploited for political gains, further exacerbating tensions and hindering genuine efforts to foster communal harmony.

The Krishna Janmabhoomi case serves as a microcosm of the broader challenges faced by India in navigating religious diversity and fostering communal harmony. Its legal journey reflects the intricate intersections of history, faith, and law, with implications that extend beyond the courtroom. As the nation grapples with the complexities of such disputes, the Krishna Janmabhoomi case underscores the urgent need for sustained efforts toward dialogue, understanding, and reconciliation for the sake of building a harmonious and inclusive society.

A. In-depth analysis of legal proceedings and judgments

The legal proceedings and judgments surrounding the Krishna Janmabhoomi dispute have evolved over the years, marked by a series of complex cases that have shaped the trajectory of the dispute. The intricate interplay of historical narratives, religious beliefs, and legal principles has rendered this legal saga both challenging and significant.

1. Early Legal Initiatives (1968-1970):

The legal journey commenced in 1968 when the Shri Krishna Janmasthan Seva Sansthan, a Hindu trust, filed a civil suit in the Mathura District Court. This suit sought the removal of the Shahi Idgah Mosque and the restoration of the site to Hindu ownership. In response, a counter-suit was filed in 1970 on behalf of the Shahi Idgah Management Committee, representing the Muslim community. These early legal initiatives set the stage for a protracted legal battle over the ownership and status of the disputed site.

2. 1989 Mathura District Court Ruling:

A significant development occurred in 1989 when a local judge ruled in favor of the Hindus, ordering the removal of a mosque that stood adjacent to the Krishna Janmabhoomi. The judge's decision favored the Hindu claim that the mosque had been built on the ruins of a Hindu temple. However, this decision was later overturned by the Allahabad High Court in 1992, citing procedural irregularities.

3. Acquisition of Certain Area at Ayodhya Act (1993):

In response to the complex and sensitive nature of religious disputes, including the Krishna Janmabhoomi case, the Indian government enacted the Acquisition of Certain Area at Ayodhya Act in 1993. This legislation aimed to acquire disputed land in Ayodhya and Mathura, freezing the legal status of both sites and maintaining the status quo.

The Act sought to provide a legal framework for preserving the existing situation to avoid further tensions.

4. Post-Ayodhya Verdict Developments (2019):

The legal landscape surrounding the Krishna Janmabhoomi dispute gained renewed attention after the Ayodhya verdict in 2019. The judgment, which favored the construction of a Ram temple at the disputed site in Ayodhya, set a precedent for similar disputes, including the one in Mathura. The judgment underscored the significance of faith and belief in determining ownership rights over disputed religious sites.

5. Current Legal Landscape:

As of the latest available information, the Krishna Janmabhoomi dispute continues to be entangled in legal intricacies. Various parties representing both Hindu and Muslim communities present their arguments and evidence to establish their claims. The legal proceedings are characterized by the challenge of reconciling historical claims with contemporary legal principles and addressing the complexities arising from the lack of definitive historical evidence.

The legal proceedings and judgments in the Krishna Janmabhoomi dispute reflect the intricate challenges inherent in resolving religiously sensitive disputes. The evolution of the legal landscape, from early civil suits to the post-Ayodhya verdict developments, highlights the multifaceted nature of this case. As the legal journey continues, it underscores the need for a nuanced and equitable resolution that respects the rights and sentiments of all parties involved, while also addressing the broader societal implications of such disputes in the context of India's diverse cultural and religious tapestry.

B. <u>Examination of archaeological and historical evidence</u>

The Krishna Janmabhoomi dispute, like many historical and religious conflicts, involves a nuanced examination of archaeological and historical evidence. The complex nature of the dispute is compounded by the lack of conclusive proof, making it a challenging task to establish a definitive narrative. However, scholars, archaeologists, and historians have delved into available evidence to contribute to the understanding of the site's history.

1. Archaeological Excavations:

Archaeological excavations at the Krishna Janmabhoomi site have been limited, and the available findings are subject to interpretation. Unlike the Ayodhya dispute, where extensive archaeological work played a pivotal role in the legal proceedings, the archaeological evidence in the Mathura case is not as comprehensive. This scarcity of direct archaeological evidence makes it challenging to draw definitive conclusions about the existence or nature of a pre-existing Hindu temple at the disputed site.

2. Historical References:

The historical references to the Krishna Janmabhoomi site date back to ancient texts and scriptures. The city of Mathura itself has been a significant center in Hindu mythology and is revered as the birthplace of Lord Krishna. While these historical references establish the religious and cultural importance of Mathura, they do not necessarily provide concrete evidence regarding the existence of a temple at the specific disputed site during the Mughal era.

3. MUGHAL ARCHITECTURE and Epigraphy:

The construction of the Shahi Idgah Mosque during the Mughal era is well-documented. Mughal architectural styles and epigraphic inscriptions can provide insights into the motivations behind the construction of the mosque. However, these features do not inherently resolve the question of whether a Hindu temple stood at the site before the mosque's construction. Interpretations of these elements may vary, and historical context plays a crucial role in shaping these interpretations.

4. Legal Implications:

The legal proceedings in the Krishna Janmabhoomi dispute have involved a careful consideration of available archaeological and historical evidence. Courts have assessed the validity and relevance of claims made by both parties based on the historical context and the weight of the evidence presented. The absence of conclusive proof has necessitated a delicate balance between acknowledging religious beliefs and applying legal principles.

5. Challenges and Interpretations:

One of the significant challenges in examining archaeological and historical evidence in the Krishna Janmabhoomi dispute is the potential for multiple interpretations. Different scholars and experts may interpret the available evidence in varying ways, influenced by their perspectives and methodologies. This subjectivity introduces an additional layer of complexity to an already intricate legal and historical landscape.

6. Ongoing Research and Dialogue:

The examination of archaeological and historical evidence in the Krishna Janmabhoomi case remains an evolving process. Ongoing research, scholarly contributions, and interdisciplinary dialogue play crucial roles in refining our understanding of the site's history. The complexities of the case highlight the importance of continued academic exploration and unbiased investigation.

The examination of archaeological and historical evidence in the Krishna Janmabhoomi dispute is a multifaceted endeavor. The scarcity of direct archaeological findings and the interpretative nature of historical references pose challenges in establishing a conclusive narrative. As legal proceedings unfold and scholars contribute to the discourse, the quest for a nuanced understanding of the site's history continues to be an integral aspect of the broader conversation surrounding this contentious issue.

C. Exploration of public sentiments and political influences

The Krishna Janmabhoomi dispute, steeped in historical and religious significance, is deeply intertwined with public sentiments and political influences, shaping the contours of the ongoing controversy. The interplay between these factors contributes to the complexity of the dispute and its resonance within the larger social and political landscape.

1. Public Sentiments:

The public sentiments surrounding the Krishna Janmabhoomi dispute are highly emotive, particularly among the Hindu community. The belief that the disputed site is the birthplace of Lord Krishna imbues it with profound religious and cultural significance. Devotees view the site as sacred, and any perceived infringement upon it is met with strong emotional reactions. These sentiments are not confined to Mathura alone but reverberate across the broader Hindu community, creating a sense of collective attachment to the site.

On the Muslim side, sentiments are shaped by the historical narrative associated with the construction of the Shahi Idgah Mosque. While religious sentiments are involved, the emotional connection to the site may differ compared to the intense religious fervor observed among Hindus.

2. Political Influences:

The Krishna Janmabhoomi dispute has been a focal point for political maneuvering and discourse. Various political entities have sought to leverage the issue to mobilize support from their respective constituencies. The political narrative surrounding the dispute often intersects with broader ideologies and agendas, contributing to the polarization of public opinion.

A. POLITICAL MOBILIZATION:

Political leaders, particularly those aligned with Hindu nationalist ideologies, have championed the cause of the Krishna Janmabhoomi, portraying it as a symbol of religious identity and cultural pride. This mobilization has been instrumental in galvanizing support, with the dispute becoming a rallying point for certain political movements.

b. Interplay with Ayodhya Verdict:

The Ayodhya verdict in 2019, which favored the construction of a Ram temple at the disputed site in Ayodhya, had a ripple effect on the Krishna Janmabhoomi dispute. The legal and political developments in Ayodhya reignited discussions and expectations regarding other contested religious sites, including Mathura. This interplay has further intensified the political dimensions of the Krishna Janmabhoomi dispute.

3. Communal Relations:

The public sentiments and political influences surrounding the Krishna Janmabhoomi dispute have had a profound impact on communal relations. The heightened emotions and political posturing have, at times, strained interfaith relationships in the region. Instances of communal tension, especially during significant legal developments, underscore the delicate balance required to navigate the complexities of religious diversity.

4. Need for Dialogue:

The polarization of public sentiments and political influences underscores the pressing need for constructive dialogue. Interfaith initiatives and efforts to facilitate understanding between different communities become imperative in mitigating tensions. Genuine dialogue can play a crucial role in fostering a sense of shared citizenship and promoting coexistence amid the deeply rooted sentiments associated with the Krishna Janmabhoomi.

5. Implications for Governance:

The Krishna Janmabhoomi dispute also poses governance challenges for local and national authorities. Balancing the protection of religious sentiments with the principles of law and order requires a nuanced approach. Political influences on governance structures can impact decision-making processes, necessitating a careful consideration of both legal and sociopolitical dimensions.

The Krishna Janmabhoomi dispute represents a confluence of deeply entrenched public sentiments and political influences. Navigating the intricacies of this complex issue requires a holistic approach that acknowledges religious beliefs while upholding the principles of secular governance. The exploration of public sentiments and political influences sheds light on the multifaceted nature of the dispute, emphasizing the importance of fostering inclusive dialogue and understanding for lasting resolution.

D. International perspectives on religious heritage and conflicts

The Krishna Janmabhoomi dispute, while rooted in the historical and religious context of India, aligns with broader international discussions on religious heritage and conflicts. The interplay of religious sentiments, cultural heritage, and legal complexities in such disputes resonates on the global stage, prompting reflections on how societies worldwide address similar challenges.

1. UNESCO and Cultural Heritage:

The United Nations Educational, Scientific and Cultural Organization (UNESCO) plays a significant role in framing international perspectives on religious heritage. UNESCO's mission includes the protection and preservation of cultural and religious sites, recognizing their universal value. Disputes over religious sites, such as the Krishna Janmabhoomi, raise questions about the role of international bodies like UNESCO in safeguarding heritage and mediating conflicts to ensure respect for diverse cultural and religious identities.

2. Interfaith Dialogue and Diplomacy:

International perspectives emphasize the importance of interfaith dialogue as a tool for conflict resolution. Recognizing the significance of religious heritage to various communities, global initiatives promote dialogue between different religious groups. Diplomacy that fosters understanding and respect for diverse religious traditions becomes essential in navigating conflicts over sacred sites, contributing to a more peaceful coexistence.

3. Legal Frameworks and Human Rights:

International human rights frameworks often address the right to freedom of religion and the protection of cultural heritage. The Krishna Janmabhoomi dispute invites considerations of how legal principles outlined in international agreements, such as the Universal Declaration of Human Rights, can guide the resolution of conflicts related to religious sites. Balancing the right to practice one's religion with the preservation of cultural heritage is a challenge faced not only by India but by nations globally.

4. Comparative Analysis of Religious Conflicts:

International perspectives benefit from a comparative analysis of religious conflicts worldwide. Examining how different nations manage disputes over religious heritage provides insights into diverse approaches and potential solutions. The Krishna Janmabhoomi dispute, in this context, becomes part of a broader conversation about the complexities inherent in preserving religious heritage within a framework of multiculturalism.

5. Role of International Community in Mediation:

International organizations and diplomatic channels can play a constructive role in mediating conflicts related to religious heritage. The Krishna Janmabhoomi dispute underscores the importance of global cooperation in facilitating dialogues and offering mediation mechanisms. The international community can contribute to creating an environment that encourages respectful engagement and understanding among diverse religious and cultural groups.

6. Religious Freedom and Pluralism:

The Krishna Janmabhoomi case prompts reflections on the broader principles of religious freedom and pluralism. International perspectives emphasize the need to uphold the right of individuals and communities to practice their religion freely while promoting an inclusive society that respects religious diversity. Resolving conflicts over religious heritage requires a commitment to fostering environments where multiple faiths can coexist harmoniously.

7. Lessons Learned for Global Harmony:

The Krishna Janmabhoomi dispute provides lessons that can inform global efforts toward religious harmony. By understanding the complexities of this dispute and its impact on communal relations, the international community can work collaboratively to develop strategies that mitigate tensions and promote respect for religious and cultural diversity.

The Krishna Janmabhoomi dispute offers a lens through which to examine international perspectives on religious heritage and conflicts. The complexities faced by India resonate with global challenges, highlighting the importance of shared principles, cross-cultural understanding, and diplomatic efforts in addressing conflicts related to religious sites and heritage. The lessons learned from such disputes contribute to the ongoing discourse on fostering peaceful coexistence in a world marked by religious and cultural diversity.

VI. Krishna Janmabhumi History

The history of Krishna Janmabhoomi is deeply embedded in the religious and cultural tapestry of India, particularly in the city of Mathura, Uttar Pradesh. The site is believed to be the birthplace of Lord Krishna, a revered deity in Hinduism. However, the historical narrative is marked by significant events, including the construction of the Shahi Idgah Mosque and the purported demolition of an earlier Hindu temple.

1. Ancient Significance:

Mathura has been a significant center of ancient Indian civilization and holds immense religious importance in Hinduism. The city is celebrated as the birthplace of Lord Krishna, who is revered as a divine figure and a central character in the Hindu epic, the Mahabharata. The cultural richness and spiritual significance of Mathura have made it a focal point for pilgrims and devotees throughout history.

2. Mughal Era and Construction of Shahi Idgah Mosque:

The turning point in the history of Krishna Janmabhoomi occurred during the Mughal era, specifically during the reign of Emperor Aurangzeb in the 17th century. In 1669, Aurangzeb ordered the construction of the Shahi Idgah Mosque in Mathura. The mosque was built adjacent to the Krishna Janmabhoomi site, and historical accounts suggest that it involved the demolition of a pre-existing Hindu temple.

3. Demolition of the Hindu Temple:

The construction of the Shahi Idgah Mosque is associated with the demolition of an earlier Hindu temple believed to be the birthplace of Lord Krishna. The exact details of the temple's architecture and historical significance remain a subject of debate, with limited archaeological evidence available to reconstruct its exact form. The demolition of the temple during the Mughal era became a point of contention and laid the foundation for the subsequent disputes over the site.

4. Iconoclasm during Aurangzeb's Reign:

The construction of the Shahi Idgah Mosque is part of a broader policy of religious iconoclasm pursued by Emperor Aurangzeb. During his reign, Aurangzeb ordered the destruction of several Hindu temples and the imposition of a more orthodox form of Islam. This policy not only altered the religious landscape of Mathura but also left a lasting impact on Hindu-Muslim relations in the region.

5. Subsequent Disputes and Legal Battles:

The events surrounding the construction of the Shahi Idgah Mosque and the purported demolition of the Hindu temple laid the foundation for the Krishna Janmabhoomi dispute. In subsequent centuries, legal battles emerged as various parties sought to establish ownership and status of the site. The lack of conclusive archaeological evidence and the intertwining of religious sentiments with legal complexities have made the dispute a longstanding and complex issue.

6. Contemporary Significance:

In contemporary times, the Krishna Janmabhoomi site remains a subject of legal and social significance. The debates surrounding the history of the site, the construction of the mosque, and the potential existence of a pre-existing Hindu temple continue to shape public discourse and legal proceedings. The historical layers of the Krishna Janmabhoomi contribute to the broader narrative of India's cultural and religious heritage.

The history of Krishna Janmabhoomi is a mosaic of ancient religious significance, the impact of the Mughal era, and the subsequent disputes over the construction of the Shahi Idgah Mosque. The events of the past continue to resonate in contemporary discussions, making the Krishna Janmabhoomi site a symbol of historical, religious, and legal complexities.

A. EVOLUTION OF KRISHNA Janmabhoomi as a religious site

The evolution of Krishna Janmabhoomi as a religious site is deeply rooted in the cultural and spiritual history of India. The significance of Mathura, the city where Lord Krishna is believed to have been born, has transformed over the centuries, shaping it into a revered pilgrimage destination for millions of Hindus.

1. Ancient Roots:

The antiquity of Mathura can be traced back to ancient times, and it is mentioned in various Hindu scriptures as a sacred and culturally rich city. The association of Mathura with Lord Krishna is found in texts like the Mahabharata and the Puranas, elevating its status as a place of divine importance. The city's connection with the life and teachings of Lord Krishna laid the foundation for its evolution into a significant religious center.

2. Birthplace of Lord Krishna:

The heart of Krishna Janmabhoomi's religious significance lies in its identification as the birthplace of Lord Krishna. According to Hindu mythology, Mathura is the exact location where Lord Krishna was born to Vasudeva and Devaki. The divine birth, marked by various miraculous events, has made Mathura a sacred site of pilgrimage for devotees seeking to connect with the spiritual legacy of Lord Krishna.

3. Cultural and Spiritual Practices:

Over the centuries, Mathura has witnessed the development of rich cultural and spiritual practices associated with Lord Krishna. Temples, ashrams, and ghats along the Yamuna River have become integral to the religious landscape of the city. The celebration of festivals like Janmashtami, commemorating Lord Krishna's birth, draws pilgrims and tourists from across the country.

4. Mughal Influence and Shahi Idgah Mosque:

During the Mughal era, the dynamics of Mathura underwent a significant transformation. Emperor Aurangzeb's religious policies led to the construction of the Shahi Idgah Mosque in the proximity of the Krishna Janmabhoomi site. The construction of the mosque involved the purported demolition of a pre-existing Hindu temple, marking a period of religious iconoclasm.

5. Emergence of the Krishna Janmabhoomi Dispute:

The construction of the Shahi Idgah Mosque laid the groundwork for the Krishna Janmabhoomi dispute. The perceived desecration of the site and the alleged demolition of the temple became pivotal elements in the evolving narrative surrounding the religious significance of the Krishna Janmabhoomi. The dispute, with its legal, historical, and emotional dimensions, further emphasized the site's role as a symbol of faith and contention.

6. LEGAL BATTLES AND Recognition:

The Krishna Janmabhoomi site gained recognition in the legal realm as various parties filed cases seeking to establish ownership and rights over the disputed land. The legal battles became a testament to the enduring religious significance of the site, with devotees and religious institutions advocating for its rightful place within the broader cultural and religious heritage.

7. Contemporary Pilgrimage and Rituals:

In contemporary times, Krishna Janmabhoomi continues to attract pilgrims and tourists alike. The Kesava Deo Temple, located near the alleged birthplace of Lord Krishna, is a focal point for devotees engaging in prayers, rituals, and celebrations. The cultural vibrancy and the religious aura of the site contribute to its ongoing evolution as a dynamic religious center.

8. Symbol of Faith and Coexistence:

Krishna Janmabhoomi stands as a symbol of faith for millions of Hindus, encapsulating the spiritual essence of Lord Krishna's birth. While the dispute surrounding the site reflects historical tensions, it also presents an opportunity for dialogue, understanding, and the potential for coexistence among different religious communities.

The evolution of Krishna Janmabhoomi as a religious site reflects a continuum of cultural, spiritual, and historical dimensions. From its ancient roots in Hindu mythology to the complex dynamics of the Mughal era and the contemporary legal battles, the site has retained its position as a symbol of religious significance, drawing devotees from diverse backgrounds who seek to connect with the divine legacy of Lord Krishna.

B. Previous attempts at resolution and their outcomes

The Krishna Janmabhoomi dispute, laden with historical, religious, and cultural complexities, has seen various attempts at resolution over the years. These efforts, driven by the desire to find a peaceful and amicable solution to the longstanding dispute, have taken different forms, involving religious leaders, political figures, and legal mechanisms.

1. Interfaith Dialogues:

Interfaith dialogues have been a recurring approach to resolving the Krishna Janmabhoomi dispute. Leaders from Hindu and Muslim communities, as well as representatives of different faiths, have engaged in discussions aimed at fostering mutual understanding and exploring possibilities for coexistence. While these dialogues have played a role in promoting religious harmony, they have not resulted in a conclusive resolution of the legal and historical complexities surrounding the disputed site.

2. Negotiations and Compromises:

Negotiations and attempts at reaching compromises have been explored as a means of resolution. In some instances, community leaders and representatives from both Hindu and Muslim communities have engaged in discussions to find common ground. However, the deeply entrenched sentiments and historical grievances often complicate the negotiation process, making it challenging to arrive at mutually acceptable terms.

3. Legal Arbitration and Court-Mediation:

The legal landscape has been a central arena for attempts at resolution. Court-mediated processes and legal arbitrations have been initiated to adjudicate on the ownership and status of the Krishna Janmabhoomi site. These legal proceedings have seen various rulings and judgments, but as of the latest available information, a definitive resolution has remained elusive. The complexities of the case, coupled with the absence of conclusive archaeological evidence, have posed challenges for legal mechanisms to bring about a comprehensive and enduring solution.

4. Government Intervention and Legislation:

Governments at both the state and national levels have intervened in the Krishna Janmabhoomi dispute in attempts to address the historical tensions. However, legislative interventions, such as the Acquisition of Certain Area at Ayodhya Act in 1993, which sought to freeze the legal status of disputed religious sites, including Mathura, have not resulted in a final resolution of the Krishna Janmabhoomi dispute. Government initiatives have often faced criticism for the perceived lack of inclusivity and comprehensive engagement with all stakeholders.

5. Social and Cultural Initiatives:

Social and cultural initiatives have sought to bridge the divide between communities by emphasizing shared heritage and cultural syncretism. These initiatives have involved organizing events, exhibitions, and cultural programs to showcase the rich historical tapestry of Mathura and promote a sense of common identity. While fostering cultural understanding is crucial, the core legal and religious issues at the heart of the dispute remain unresolved.

6. Impacts of Ayodhya Verdict:

The Ayodhya verdict in 2019, which granted permission for the construction of a Ram temple at the disputed site in Ayodhya, reignited discussions and expectations surrounding other contested religious sites, including Mathura. The impact of the Ayodhya verdict has led to renewed attention on the Krishna Janmabhoomi dispute, with stakeholders exploring potential implications for the resolution of the case.

Previous attempts at resolving the Krishna Janmabhoomi dispute have involved a multifaceted approach encompassing interfaith dialogues, negotiations, legal arbitration, government interventions, and cultural initiatives. Despite these efforts, a conclusive and universally accepted resolution remains elusive, emphasizing the complexity and sensitivity of the issues surrounding the disputed site. The persistent challenges of reconciling historical narratives, religious sentiments, and legal intricacies underscore the need for sustained and inclusive efforts towards finding a lasting solution to the Krishna Janmabhoomi dispute.

C. Role of various stakeholders in the ongoing dispute

The Krishna Janmabhoomi dispute involves a diverse array of stakeholders, each playing a distinct role in shaping the narrative and influencing the trajectory of the ongoing conflict. These stakeholders include religious leaders, political figures, legal authorities, community representatives, and the general public, all of whom contribute to the complex dynamics surrounding the disputed site in Mathura.

1. Hindu Religious Leaders and Devotees:

Hindu religious leaders, representing various sects and organizations, play a pivotal role in advocating for the rights and interests of the Hindu community in the Krishna Janmabhoomi dispute. They often articulate the religious significance of the site, emphasizing its sanctity as the birthplace of Lord Krishna. Devotees, influenced by the guidance of these leaders, form a crucial part of the stakeholder group, expressing their deep emotional and spiritual connection to the Krishna Janmabhoomi.

2. Muslim Community Representatives:

Representatives of the Muslim community are essential stakeholders in the dispute, particularly concerning the contested Shahi Idgah Mosque. Muslim leaders and organizations engage in discussions and legal proceedings to assert the rights and interests of the Muslim community in relation to the disputed site. The dynamics of the dispute require a delicate balance between the concerns of both religious communities.

3. Legal Authorities and Courts:

The judiciary, including local courts and higher judicial bodies, plays a critical role in adjudicating the Krishna Janmabhoomi dispute. Legal authorities assess the historical and legal claims put forth by the parties involved and make decisions that have far-reaching implications. Court judgments, such as those related to ownership and status, shape the legal framework within which the dispute unfolds.

4. Political Figures and Government Authorities:

Political figures and government authorities, both at the state and national levels, exert influence on the Krishna Janmabhoomi dispute. Government interventions, legislations, and policies can significantly impact the resolution process. The historical and political context of the dispute often sees political figures aligning with specific communities or ideologies, further complicating the already sensitive dynamics.

5. Community Organizations and NGOs:

Various community organizations and non-governmental organizations (NGOs) actively engage in the Krishna Janmabhoomi dispute. These entities work to represent the interests of their respective communities, facilitate dialogue, and contribute to social and cultural initiatives aimed at fostering understanding. Their involvement underscores the broader societal implications of the dispute.

6. Interfaith Initiatives:

Interfaith initiatives and organizations that promote dialogue and understanding between different religious communities play a constructive role in the Krishna Janmabhoomi dispute. These efforts aim to bridge the gap between Hindus and Muslims, encouraging mutual respect and coexistence. Interfaith leaders often act as mediators, facilitating discussions and fostering an atmosphere of inclusivity.

7. Academic and Archaeological Experts:

Academic and archaeological experts contribute to the dispute by providing insights based on historical research and archaeological findings. Their assessments of the site's history, including the existence of a pre-existing temple, inform the legal and public discourse surrounding the Krishna Janmabhoomi. However, interpretations of evidence may vary, adding complexity to the ongoing discussions.

8. Public Sentiment and Civil Society:

The general public, influenced by religious, cultural, and historical sentiments, forms a crucial part of the stakeholder group. Public sentiment can shape the narrative, and civil society plays a role in advocating for peaceful coexistence and resolution. Grassroots movements, public demonstrations, and awareness campaigns contribute to the broader societal impact of the Krishna Janmabhoomi dispute.

The Krishna Janmabhoomi dispute involves a diverse array of stakeholders, each with their own perspectives, interests, and roles. Navigating the complexities of this dispute requires a nuanced understanding of the contributions and influences of these stakeholders, as they collectively shape the ongoing narrative surrounding the contested site in Mathura.

VII. Current Case Update of Krishna Janmabhoomi

A. Recent developments in the legal proceedings

The Krishna Janmabhumi dispute has been a long standing and complex legal matter, marked by various legal proceedings and court decisions over the years. The dispute primarily revolves around the claim to the site believed to be the birthplace of Lord Krishna, with both Hindu and Muslim communities asserting their rights over the land.

One of the critical legal milestones in the Krishna Janmabhoomi dispute was the acquisition of certain areas in Mathura, including the disputed site, by the government under the Acquisition of Certain Area at Ayodhya Act, 1993. This legislation aimed at freezing the legal status of disputed religious sites, preventing any alteration in their character.

In recent years, there has been a renewed focus on the Krishna Janmabhumi dispute in the wake of the Ayodhya verdict in 2019. The Ayodhya verdict, delivered by the Supreme Court of India, resolved the contentious Ayodhya land dispute by allocating the disputed site for the construction of a Ram temple and providing an alternative plot for a mosque. This development sparked discussions and expectations surrounding other disputed religious sites, including Mathura.

The legal proceedings related to Krishna Janmabhumi involve complex questions of historical evidence, archaeological findings, and religious sentiments. Both Hindu and Muslim organizations have been actively involved in presenting their cases, and the courts have faced the challenging task of reconciling these divergent claims.

Efforts have been made by various stakeholders, including interfaith groups and community leaders, to facilitate dialogue and find amicable solutions. However, the deeply rooted religious sentiments and historical narratives have made the resolution of the Krishna Janmabhumi dispute a complex and sensitive matter.

It is essential to check recent and reliable news sources or official court records for the most up-to-date information on developments in the legal proceedings of Krishna Janmabhumi. Legal cases can see new filings, court hearings, or judgments, and staying informed through authoritative channels is crucial to understanding the current status of the dispute.

B. Government initiatives or interventions

The Krishna Janmabhumi dispute has witnessed various government initiatives and interventions over the years, reflecting the state's role in managing and attempting to resolve complex religious and cultural conflicts. While the dispute primarily involves legal and historical aspects, government interventions have played a significant role in shaping the narrative and seeking avenues for resolution.

1. Acquisition of Certain Area at Ayodhya Act, 1993:

One of the crucial legislative interventions related to disputed religious sites, including Krishna Janmabhumi, is the Acquisition of Certain Area at Ayodhya Act, 1993. This legislation aimed to freeze the status quo of religious places as it existed on August 15, 1947. By doing so, it prevented any alteration in the character of the disputed sites, including the one in Mathura. The Act was enacted in response to the Ayodhya dispute and sought to address similar conflicts at other locations.

2. Political Positions and Policy Implications:

Governments at both the state and national levels have often taken positions on the Krishna Janmabhumi dispute, reflecting the political landscape and ideologies of the ruling parties. Political figures have articulated their stances on the issue, influencing public perception and contributing to the broader socio political context surrounding the dispute. Policy implications, whether through legislative actions or administrative decisions, have shaped the trajectory of the dispute.

3. Ayodhya Verdict and Potential Ramifications:

The Ayodhya verdict in 2019, which addressed the Ram Janmabhoomi-Babri Masjid land dispute, has reverberated in discussions about other contested religious sites, including Krishna Janmabhumi. The government's response to the Ayodhya verdict and its potential implications for similar disputes have been topics of public discourse. The legal and political consequences of the Ayodhya judgment have been considered within the broader framework of religious disputes in India.

4. Calls for Legislative Action:

In certain instances, there have been calls for legislative action to address the Krishna Janmabhumi dispute. Some stakeholders have advocated for specific laws or amendments to existing legislation to provide a legal framework for the resolution of religious conflicts. These proposals have been subject to debate, and the feasibility of legislative solutions in the context of the dispute remains a point of discussion.

5. Preservation of Cultural Heritage:

Government initiatives have also focused on the preservation and promotion of cultural heritage associated with Krishna Janmabhumi. Efforts to conserve historical sites, conduct archaeological research, and support cultural activities that highlight the religious and historical significance of the region have been part of broader strategies to manage the dispute and foster a sense of shared heritage.

6. Dialogue and Consultations:

At times, governments have facilitated or encouraged dialogues and consultations between different religious communities involved in the Krishna Janmabhumi dispute. Interfaith initiatives and efforts to bring various stakeholders to the negotiating table have been part of attempts to find common ground and promote understanding.

7. Balancing Communal Harmony:

Government interventions have often aimed at maintaining communal harmony and preventing tensions that could arise from religious disputes. Strategies for balancing the interests of different religious communities, ensuring the safety and security of religious sites, and fostering an atmosphere of coexistence have been integral aspects of government initiatives.

Government interventions in the Krishna Janmabhumi dispute have taken various forms, encompassing legislative actions, political positions, policy implications, and efforts to preserve cultural heritage. The complexities of the dispute demand a nuanced approach, balancing legal considerations with the imperative of maintaining communal harmony and respecting the diverse religious sentiments associated with the contested site.

C. Public reactions and protests

The Krishna Janmabhoomi dispute has not only been a legal and political matter but also a source of strong public reactions and occasional protests. The deep religious sentiments associated with the site have stirred emotions, leading to both expressions of fervent devotion and instances of communal tension.

1. Emotional Attachment and Devotion:

The disputed site in Mathura holds immense significance for millions of Hindus who consider it to be the birthplace of Lord Krishna. Devotees express their emotional attachment through pilgrimages, prayers, and rituals at the various temples in the vicinity. The perceived sanctity of the Krishna Janmabhumi has evoked a profound sense of devotion among the Hindu community, contributing to the emotional intensity surrounding the dispute.

2. Interfaith Harmony Initiatives:

While the dispute has the potential to strain interfaith relations, there have been instances of individuals and organizations promoting interfaith harmony and understanding. Initiatives focused on dialogue, cultural exchange, and shared festivities have aimed at fostering a sense of coexistence among different religious communities in the region.

3. Political Mobilization and Protests:

Political figures and organizations have often mobilized public sentiment for or against specific positions related to the Krishna Janmabhumi dispute. Protests, demonstrations, and rallies, both in support and opposition to various claims, have occurred periodically. The dispute has, at times, become a rallying point for political movements advocating for particular ideological or religious agendas.

4. Legal Judgments and Public Reaction:

Major legal judgments related to the Krishna Janmabhoomi dispute have triggered public reactions. The Ayodhya verdict in 2019, which granted permission for the construction of a Ram temple at the disputed site in Ayodhya, had implications for discussions surrounding other contested religious sites, including Mathura. Public reactions to legal developments often reflect the diverse perspectives within society.

5. Communal Tensions:

Communal tensions have, unfortunately, been part of the broader narrative surrounding the Krishna Janmabhumi dispute. Instances of clashes between different religious communities or localized tensions have been reported, underscoring the delicate nature of religious conflicts and the potential for discord when emotions run high.

6. Social Media Influence:

The advent of social media has amplified public discourse on the Krishna Janmabhumi dispute. Debates, opinions, and reactions are shared widely, contributing to the shaping of public sentiment. Social media platforms serve as arenas for both constructive dialogue and, at times, the proliferation of divisive narratives.

7. Public Expectations and Anticipation:

Public expectations and anticipation often heighten during significant legal developments or political discussions related to the dispute. The release of court judgments, announcements by political leaders, or proposals for resolution can trigger widespread interest and reactions from the public, with communities closely monitoring the progression of the dispute.

8. Calls for Peaceful Resolution:

Amidst the passionate expressions of devotion and occasional tensions, there have been calls from various quarters for a peaceful and amicable resolution to the Krishna Janmabhumi dispute. Voices advocating for dialogue, understanding, and mutual respect seek to bridge divides and promote harmony.

In summary, public reactions and occasional protests surrounding the Krishna Janmabhumi dispute are reflective of the deep emotional and religious connections people have with the site. While some expressions are rooted in devotion and a desire for the protection of cultural heritage, there have also been instances of tension, emphasizing the need for balanced approaches and inclusive dialogue in the resolution of this sensitive matter.

D. International reactions or involvement

The Krishna Janmabhumi dispute, primarily a domestic matter within India, has not garnered significant international reactions or direct involvement from foreign governments. However, the broader context of religious disputes and heritage preservation has occasionally drawn attention and commentary from international organizations and scholars. Here are some points regarding international reactions:

1. UNESCO and Cultural Heritage:

International organizations, such as UNESCO (United Nations Educational, Scientific and Cultural Organization), focus on the preservation of cultural heritage globally. While UNESCO has not directly commented on the Krishna Janmabhumi dispute, its principles of safeguarding cultural and religious sites are relevant. The organization advocates for the protection of historical monuments and religious structures, emphasizing the importance of respecting diverse cultural identities.

2. Scholars and Academic Discussions:

The Krishna Janmabhumi dispute has been a subject of academic interest and scholarly discussions beyond India's borders. International scholars and researchers have contributed to the discourse, providing perspectives on the historical, cultural, and legal aspects of the dispute. Conferences, seminars, and academic publications have explored the complexities of religious conflicts and heritage preservation, with a few scholars offering comparative analyses with similar global situations.

3. Diplomatic Sensitivity:

Given the sensitive nature of religious disputes, there is a general understanding in international diplomatic circles about the importance of respecting the sovereignty of nations in resolving such matters. Foreign governments, particularly those with diplomatic ties to India, tend to approach issues related to religious sites with caution, recognizing the internal nature of these disputes.

4. Soft Power and Cultural Diplomacy:

Issues related to cultural and religious heritage can indirectly influence a country's image on the global stage. India, being a diverse and culturally rich nation, often employs soft power and cultural diplomacy to enhance its global standing. Events related to the Krishna Janmabhumi dispute may contribute to discussions about India's commitment to preserving its cultural heritage and managing internal diversity.

5. Religious Freedom Advocacy:

International human rights organizations and advocacy groups concerned with religious freedom may monitor situations involving disputes over religious sites. While the Krishna Janmabhumi dispute has not been a focal point for international religious freedom discussions, the broader principles of protecting individuals' right to practice their religion freely align with the concerns raised in religious disputes.

6. Indian Diaspora Engagement:

Members of the Indian diaspora may express their views on the Krishna Janmabhumi dispute, reflecting diverse perspectives and affiliations. The diaspora's engagement with the issue may include public discussions, articles, or events that contribute to a global dialogue on religious tolerance, heritage preservation, and the complexities of multicultural societies.

7. Limited Direct Involvement:

Direct involvement or intervention by foreign governments in the Krishna Janmabhumi dispute is limited. The sensitivity of religious issues and the recognition of India's sovereignty over internal matters typically guide international responses, with foreign leaders and officials refraining from direct interference in such disputes.

While the Krishna Janmabhumi dispute remains primarily a domestic issue, it intersects with broader global conversations on cultural heritage, religious freedom, and multiculturalism. International reactions are often indirect, with organizations and scholars contributing to academic discussions and global dialogues on the complexities of managing diverse cultural and religious landscapes.

Conclusion

In conclusion, the Krishna Janmabhumi dispute stands as a poignant testament to the intricate interplay of history, faith, and cultural identity in India. This multifaceted issue, revolving around the believed birthplace of Lord Krishna, has traversed legal labyrinths, stirred communal dynamics, and elicited profound emotional responses from devotees.

The dispute's ongoing significance in contemporary times is underscored by its role as a religious pilgrimage site, a cultural heritage hub, and a symbol of unity for the Hindu community. Beyond its religious connotations, Krishna Janmabhumi resonates as a source of literary and artistic inspiration, contributing to the rich tapestry of Indian culture.

However, the complexities surrounding the dispute necessitate a careful and balanced approach. The need for a peaceful resolution and communal harmony cannot be overstated. It calls for acknowledging and respecting diverse perspectives, fostering open dialogue, and ensuring fair representation within the legal framework. Interfaith initiatives, cultural preservation efforts, and educational programs can contribute to building bridges between communities, promoting understanding, and nurturing a shared sense of heritage.

In navigating the future of Krishna Janmabhumi, the delicate task lies in weaving together the historical layers, mythological threads, and contemporary aspirations of diverse communities. By embracing a spirit of inclusivity, governments, religious leaders, and communities can collectively work towards a resolution that honors the past, fosters communal harmony, and paves the way for a shared future.

As India continues to evolve, the Krishna Janmabhumi dispute serves as a poignant reminder of the delicate balance required in managing the rich tapestry of its cultural and religious diversity. It is a call to transcend divisions, uphold the principles of justice and understanding, and weave a narrative that reflects the unity in diversity at the heart of the nation's ethos.

A. Summarize key points

The Krishna Janmabhumi dispute is a complex tapestry woven with historical, religious, and cultural threads, centered around the belief that it is the birthplace of Lord Krishna. As we delve into the intricacies of this dispute, several key points emerge, shaping the narrative and reflecting the nuanced dynamics at play:

Historical Layers and Mythological Threads:

The site is a convergence of historical narratives and mythological beliefs, with the mythical birth of Lord Krishna entwined in the fabric of the region's history.

The challenge lies in reconciling competing narratives that span both mythological and historical dimensions, making it a unique and intricate case.

Legal Labyrinth:

The legal journey of Krishna Janmabhumi has traversed a labyrinth of courtrooms, legislations, and judgments.

From the Ayodhya Act of 1993 to various court decisions, the legal framework reflects the complexities of adjudicating matters of faith and historical significance.

Communal Dynamics and Societal Relations:

The dispute has implications for communal dynamics, occasionally leading to tensions and protests as religious identities intertwine with the site's significance.

Efforts at interfaith dialogue and initiatives fostering understanding highlight the delicate balance required in navigating religious diversity within the Indian social context.

Governmental Roles and Global Perspectives:

Government interventions, both legislative and administrative, play a pivotal role in managing religious conflicts, as seen in the Ayodhya Act and political positions.

While international perspectives remain largely indirect, global discussions on cultural heritage, religious freedom, and internal disputes contribute to the broader context.

Human Emotions and Devotion:

Devotees express deep-seated emotions and devotion to the site, undertaking pilgrimages, prayers, and rituals that transcend legal and political dimensions.

The emotional attachment reflects the profound impact of religious beliefs on individuals and communities.

Pathways to Resolution:

Resolution necessitates a delicate balancing act, considering the intertwining of mythology, history, and religious sentiments.

Dialogues, both legal and interfaith, offer potential pathways to reconciliation, recognizing shared cultural heritage as common ground for constructive discussions.

The Krishna Janmabhumi dispute encapsulates the multifaceted nature of religious conflicts, requiring nuanced approaches that respect diverse perspectives.

The quest for resolution lies in navigating intricate threads of history, law, communal dynamics, and human emotions, recognizing the evolving story of Krishna Janmabhumi.

As the dispute continues to unfold, these key points provide insights into the complexity and sensitivity surrounding the contested site in Mathura, illustrating the challenges and potential pathways towards a harmonious resolution.

B. Highlight the ongoing significance of Krishna Janmabhumi in contemporary times

The significance of Krishna Janmabhumi extends beyond historical and religious contexts, embedding itself in contemporary times with profound implications for culture, identity, and societal dynamics:

Cultural Identity and Heritage Preservation:

Krishna Janmabhumi is a cornerstone of cultural identity for millions of Hindus, serving as a symbol of their spiritual and historical heritage.

The ongoing significance lies in the collective endeavor to preserve and celebrate this cultural identity, fostering a sense of continuity and shared history.

Religious Devotion and Pilgrimage:

In contemporary times, Krishna Janmabhumi continues to attract devout Hindus who undertake pilgrimages to the site, seeking spiritual connection and divine blessings.

The ongoing significance is reflected in the continuous flow of pilgrims, reinforcing the religious devotion associated with the revered birthplace.

Symbolism for Interfaith Relations:

Krishna Janmabhumi holds symbolic importance for interfaith relations, providing an opportunity for dialogue and understanding between different religious communities.

Its ongoing significance lies in the potential to bridge divides and foster a spirit of coexistence in a multicultural society.

Tourism and Economic Impact:

The site's ongoing significance extends to the realm of tourism, contributing to the local and regional economy.

Pilgrims and tourists alike visit Krishna Janmabhumi, generating economic opportunities and promoting the cultural and historical richness of the region.

Legal Precedent and Historical Narratives:

Ongoing legal proceedings related to Krishna Janmabhumi contribute to shaping legal precedents in matters of historical and religious disputes.

The significance lies in how contemporary legal decisions can influence the broader discourse on the preservation of religious heritage.

Political Symbolism and Public Discourse:

Krishna Janmabhumi remains a political symbol, featuring in public discourse and political agendas.

Ongoing discussions and debates surrounding the site underscore its continued relevance in shaping political narratives and public opinion.

Global Recognition and Academic Interest:

The ongoing significance of Krishna Janmabhumi is also reflected in its recognition on the global stage and the interest it garners from international scholars and academics.

Academic discussions contribute to a broader understanding of the complexities surrounding religious disputes and cultural heritage preservation.

Media and Social Media Influence:

The ongoing significance of Krishna Janmabhumi is amplified by media coverage and social media influence, shaping public perceptions and discussions.

Information dissemination and public engagement continue to play a crucial role in keeping the site relevant in contemporary discourse.

In summary, Krishna Janmabhumi's ongoing significance in contemporary times is multifaceted, encompassing cultural identity, religious devotion, economic impact, legal precedent, political symbolism, and global recognition. Its role in shaping interfaith relations and fostering dialogue underscores the need for nuanced approaches to navigate the complexities associated with this revered site.

Also by Swatantra Bahadur

1. Blossom with confidence
2. "Depression: A Roller Coaster Ride"
3. Finding Your Voice
4. Rahul Gandhi: The Untold Story
5. 100 Aspects on Nature
6. Love By An Introvert
7. Breaking Barriers: LGBTQ Rights and Social Justice
8. Man Of Golden India "Narendra Modi"
9. India " Unity lies in Diversity"
10. Indian's Heritage of Kashi "Varanasi"
11. "The Power of Voice: Lawyer in a Black Coat"
12. Shri Ram Janmabhumi "Ayodhya"
13. Social Media and Youth: Navigating the Digital Landscape
14. Jai Shri Hanuman Garhi "Ayodhya"
15. Chronicles of the Multiverse Cafe
16. "Unveiling Pain: The Global Impact of COVID-19

Website - Bookwisehub.com

About the Author

Instagram Id - swatantrabahadur15

Email Id - swatantrbahadur@gmail.com

Read more at https://bookwisehub.com/.